zodiac MOUNTS 3
Coloring book

AUTHOR AND ILLUSTRATOR
OLGA GOLOVESHKINA

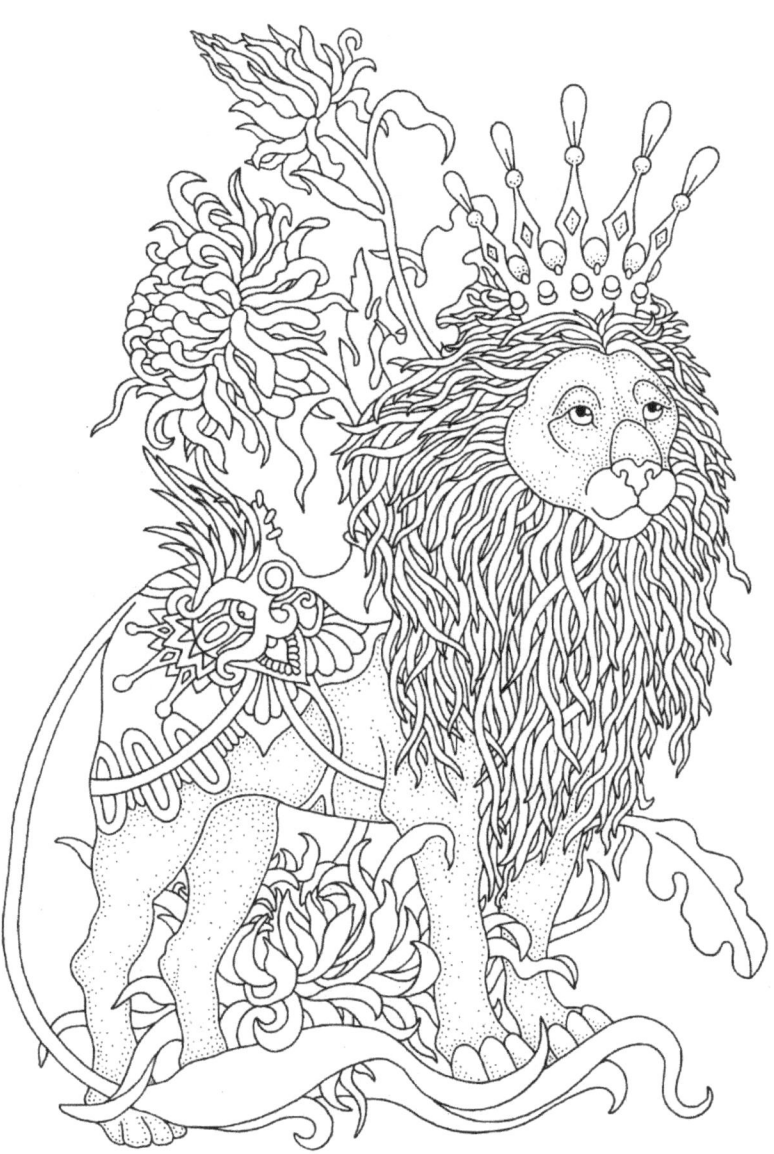

Copyright © 2017 Olga Goloveshkina

All rights reserved.

ISBN:1975632966
ISBN-13:9781975632960

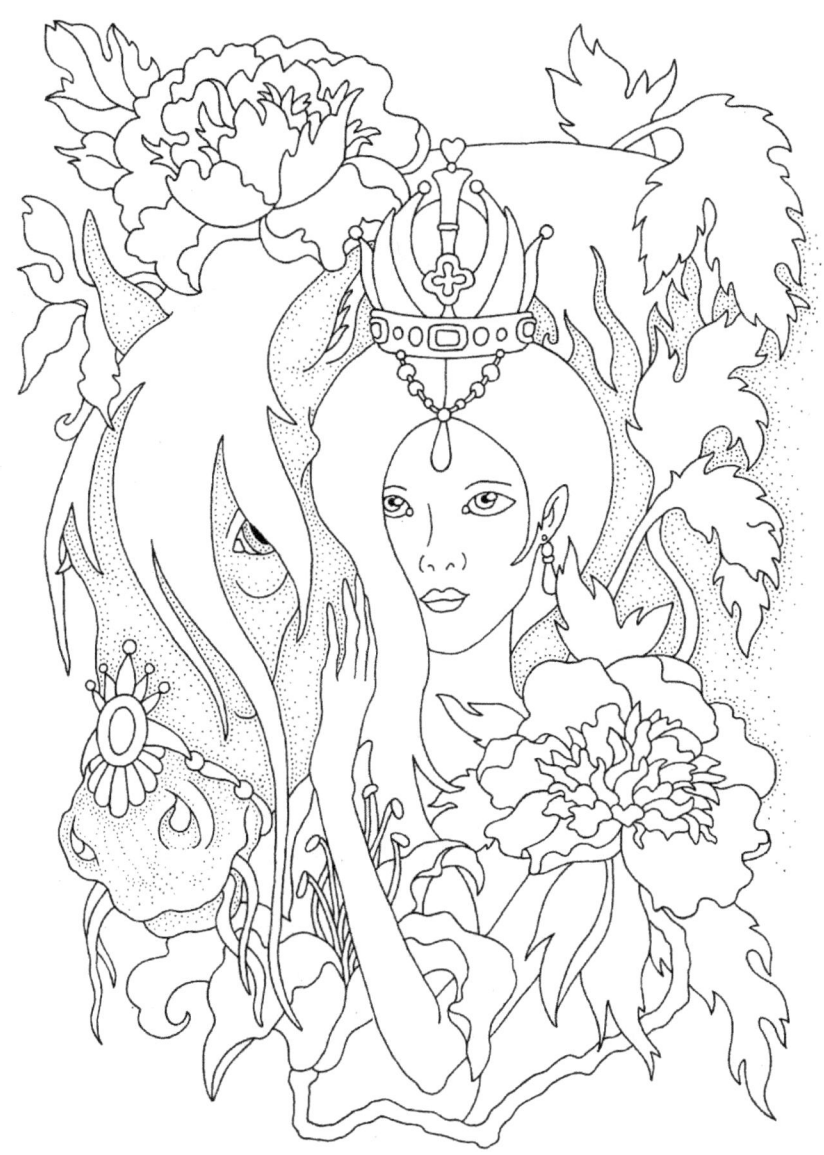

This book belongs to

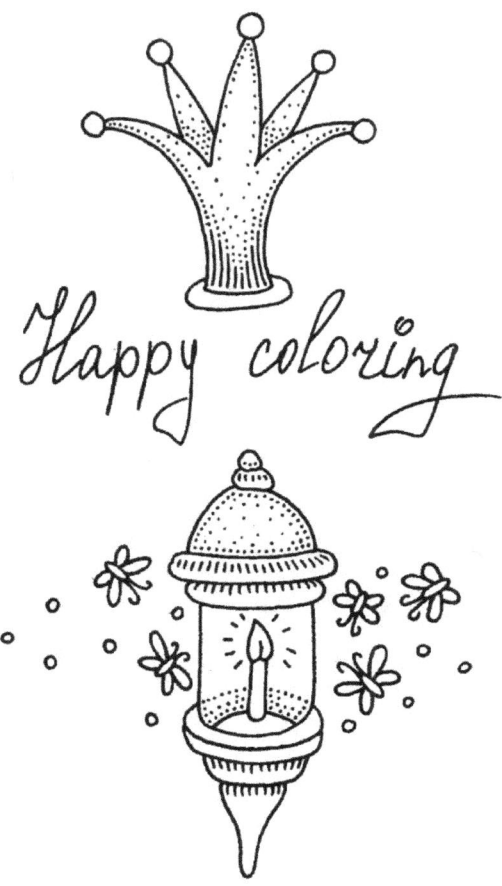

Happy coloring

Thank you for choosing my coloring book!

Olya :)

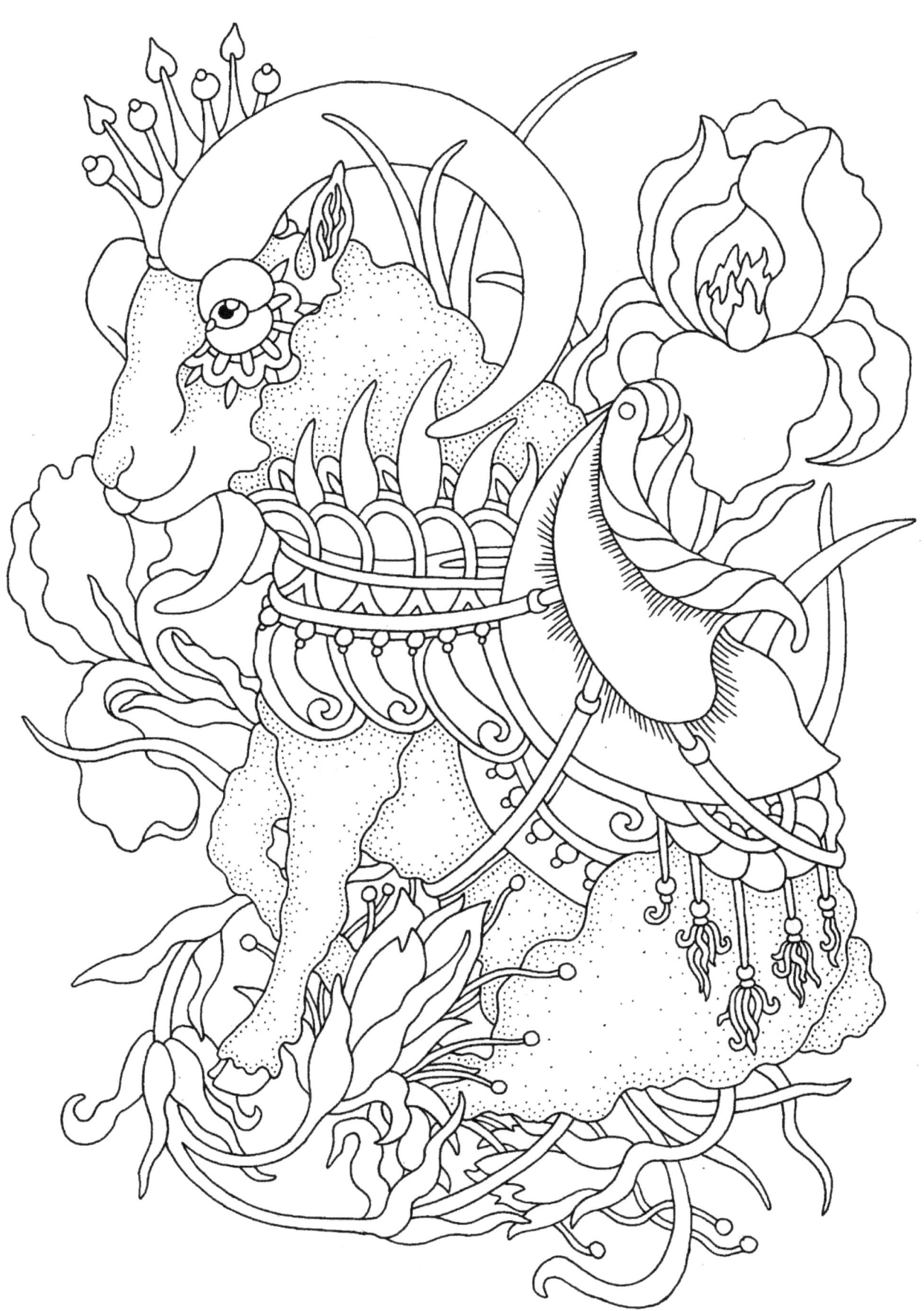

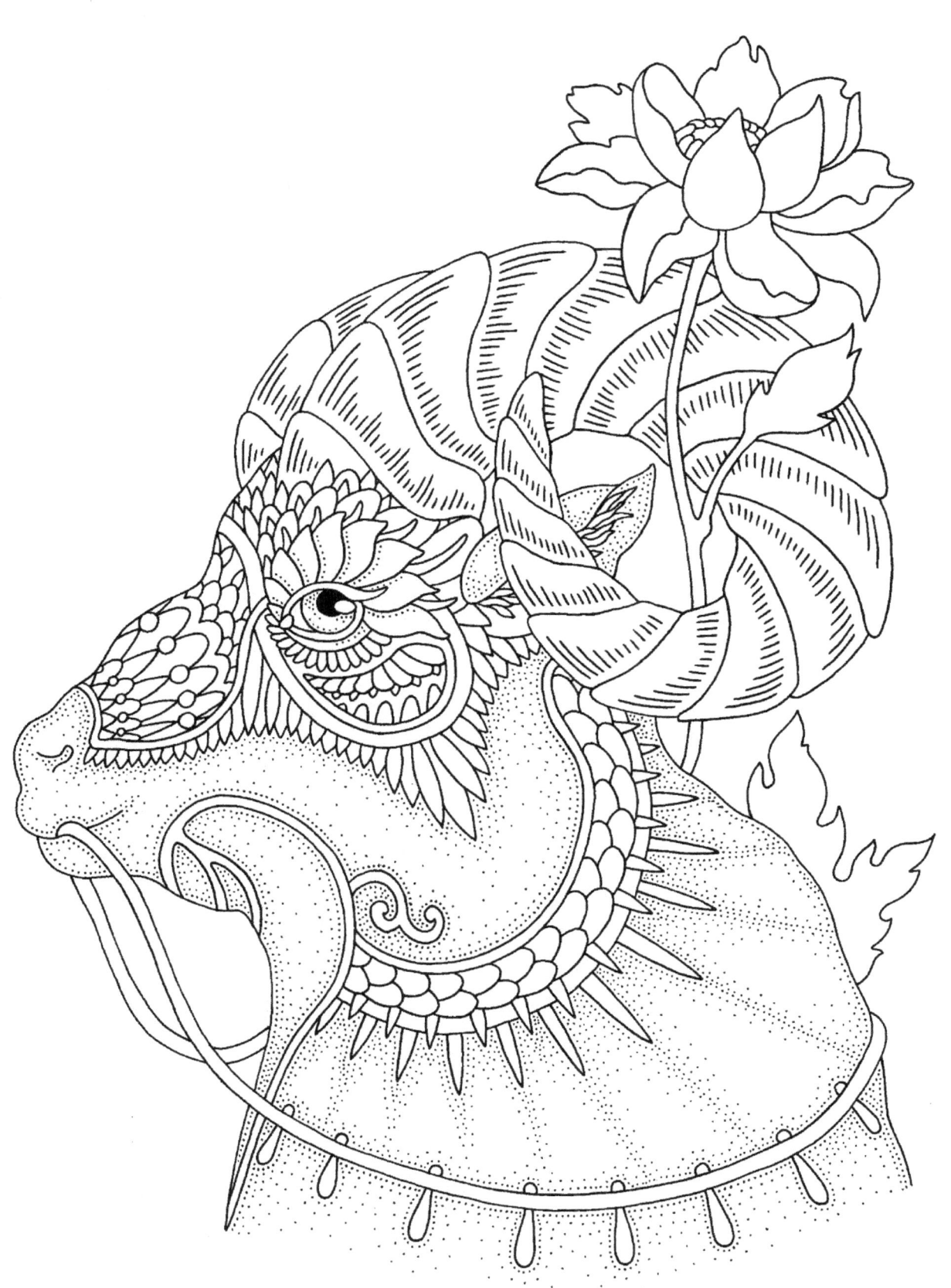

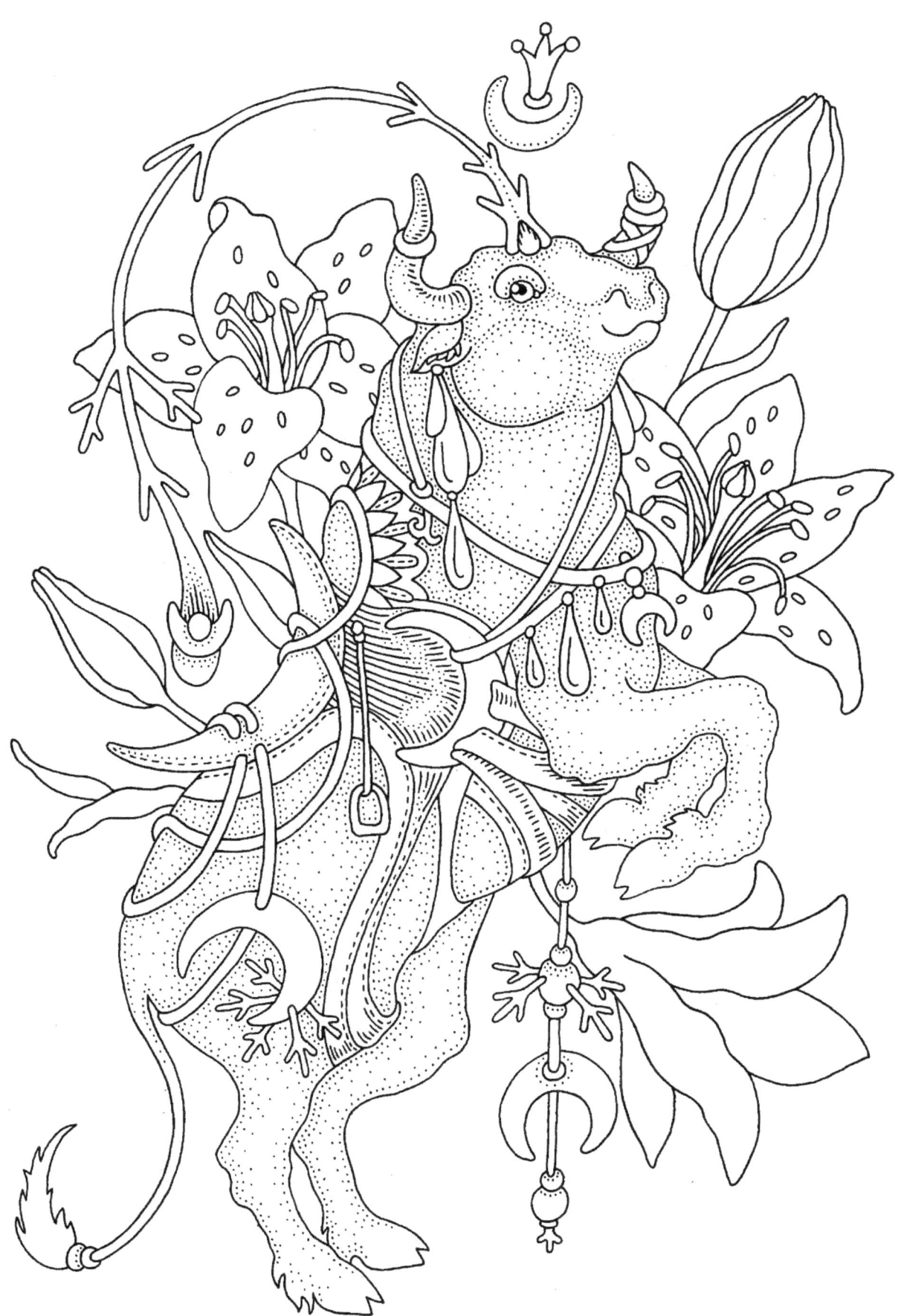

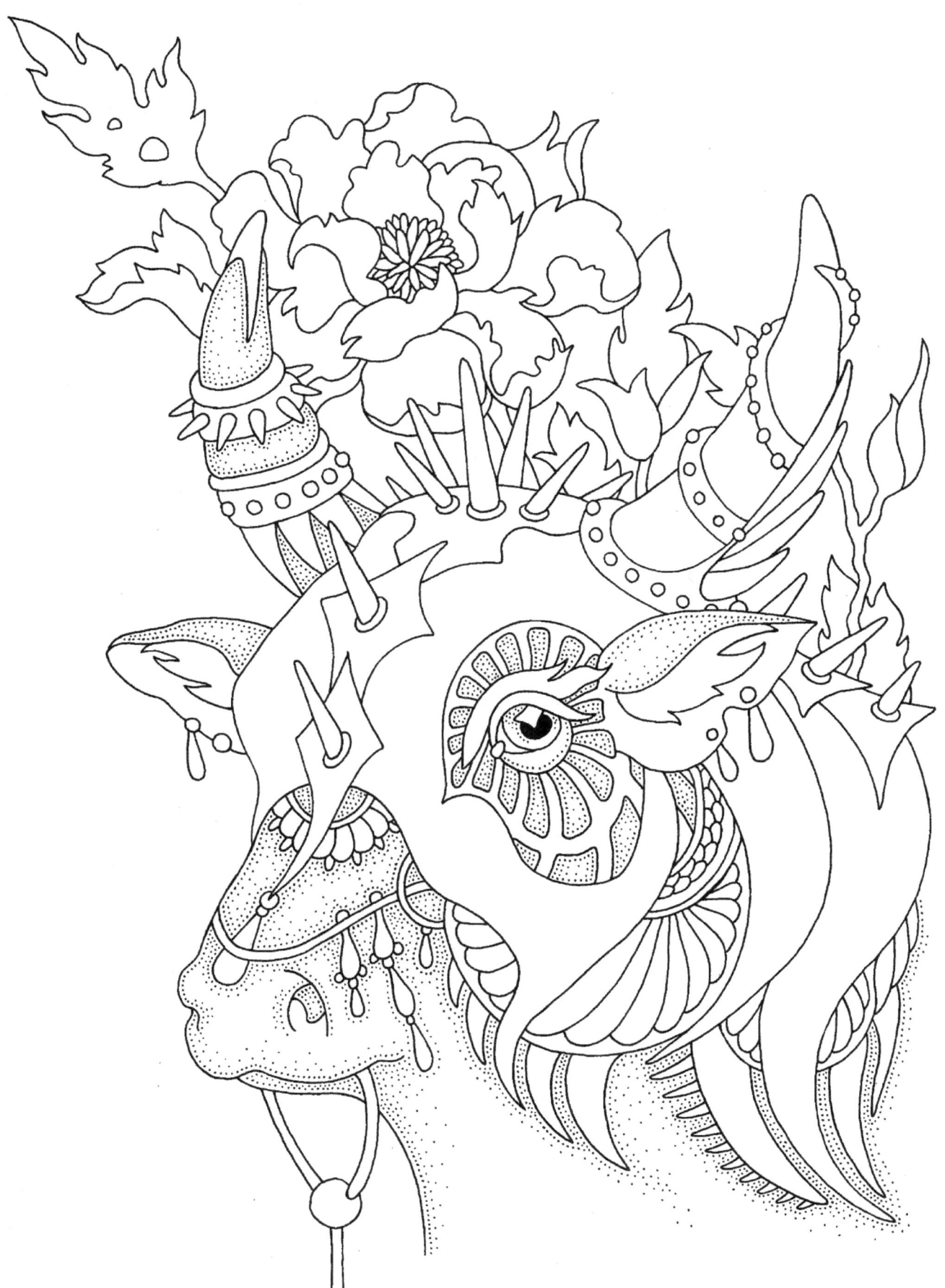

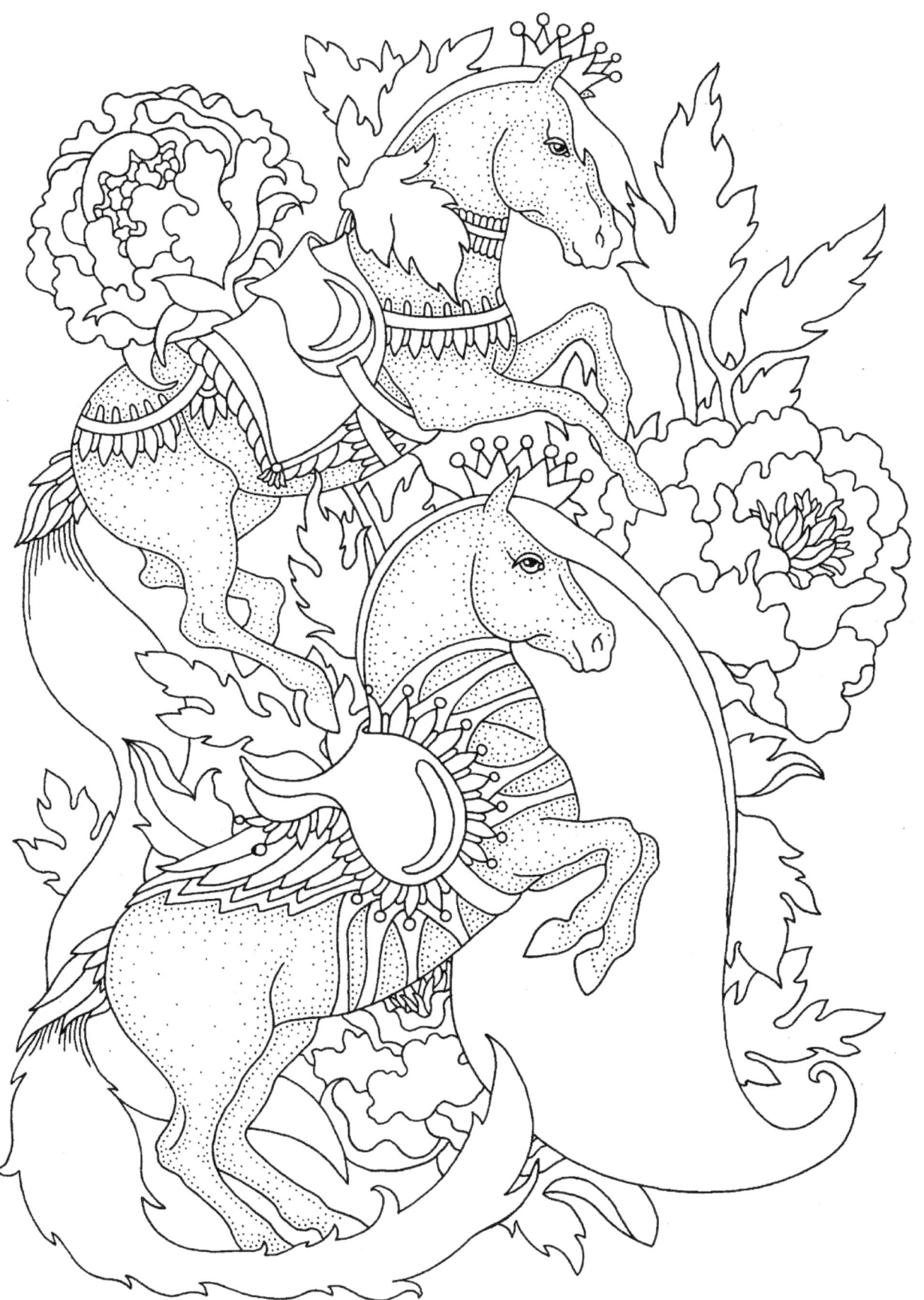

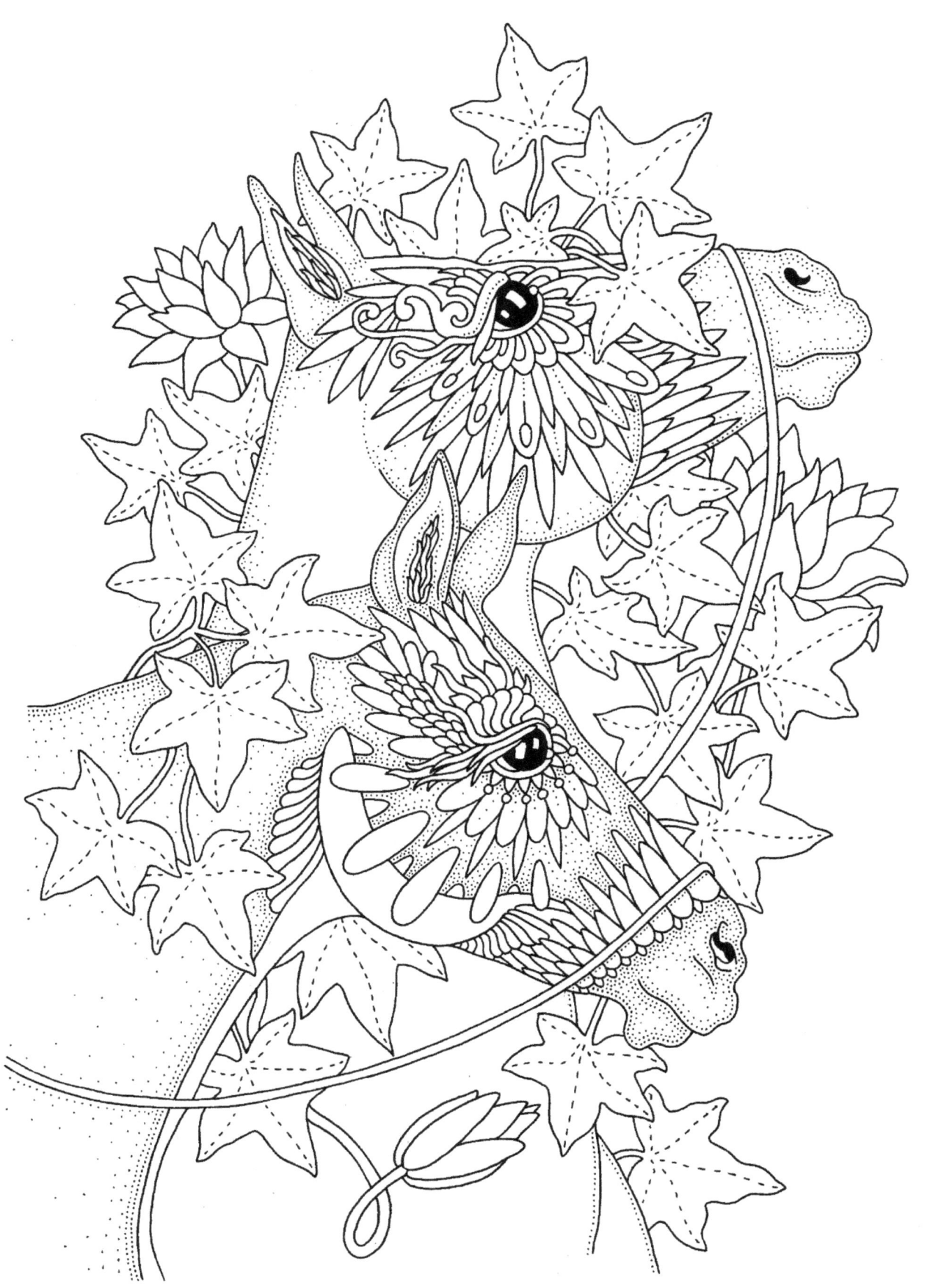

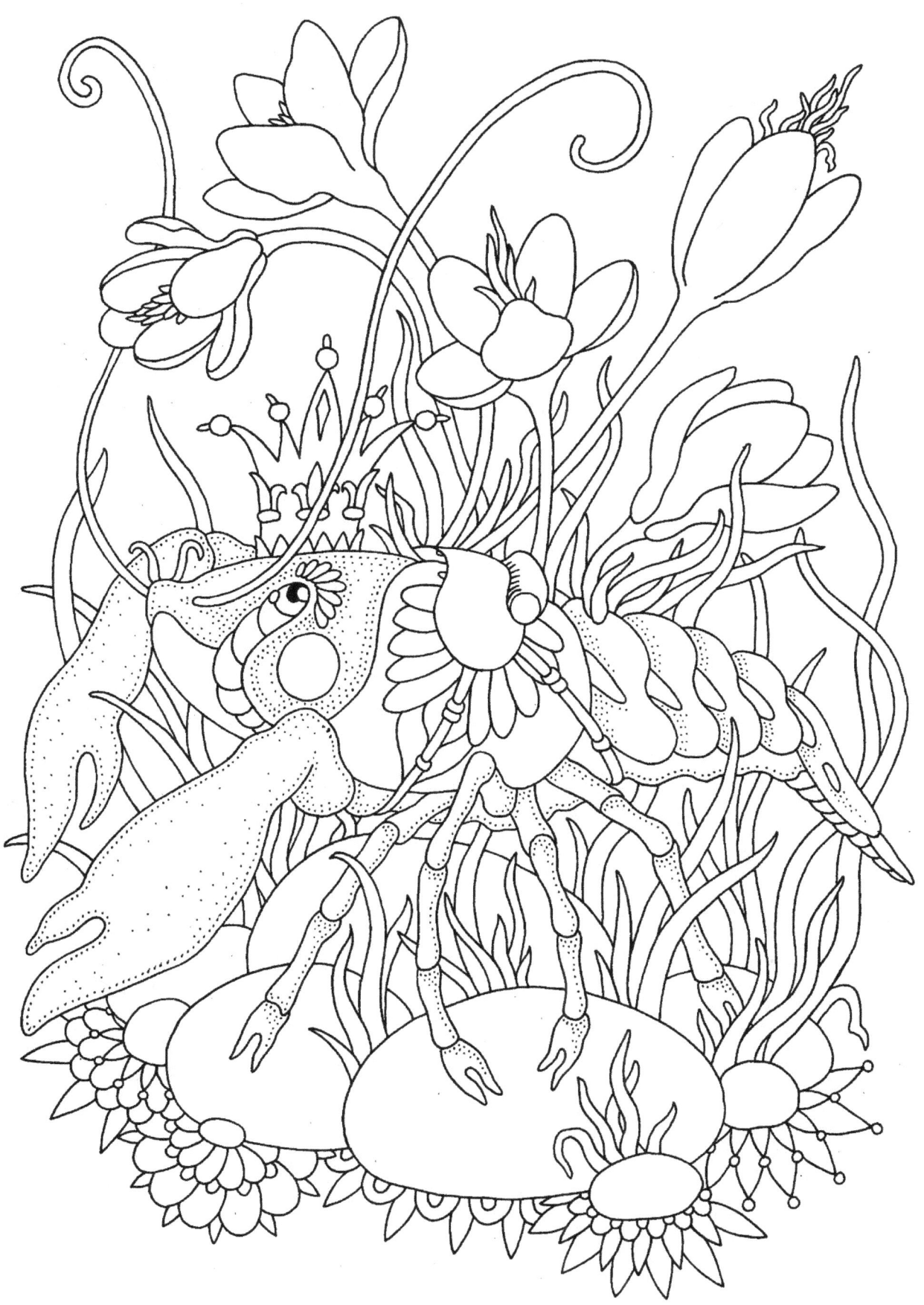

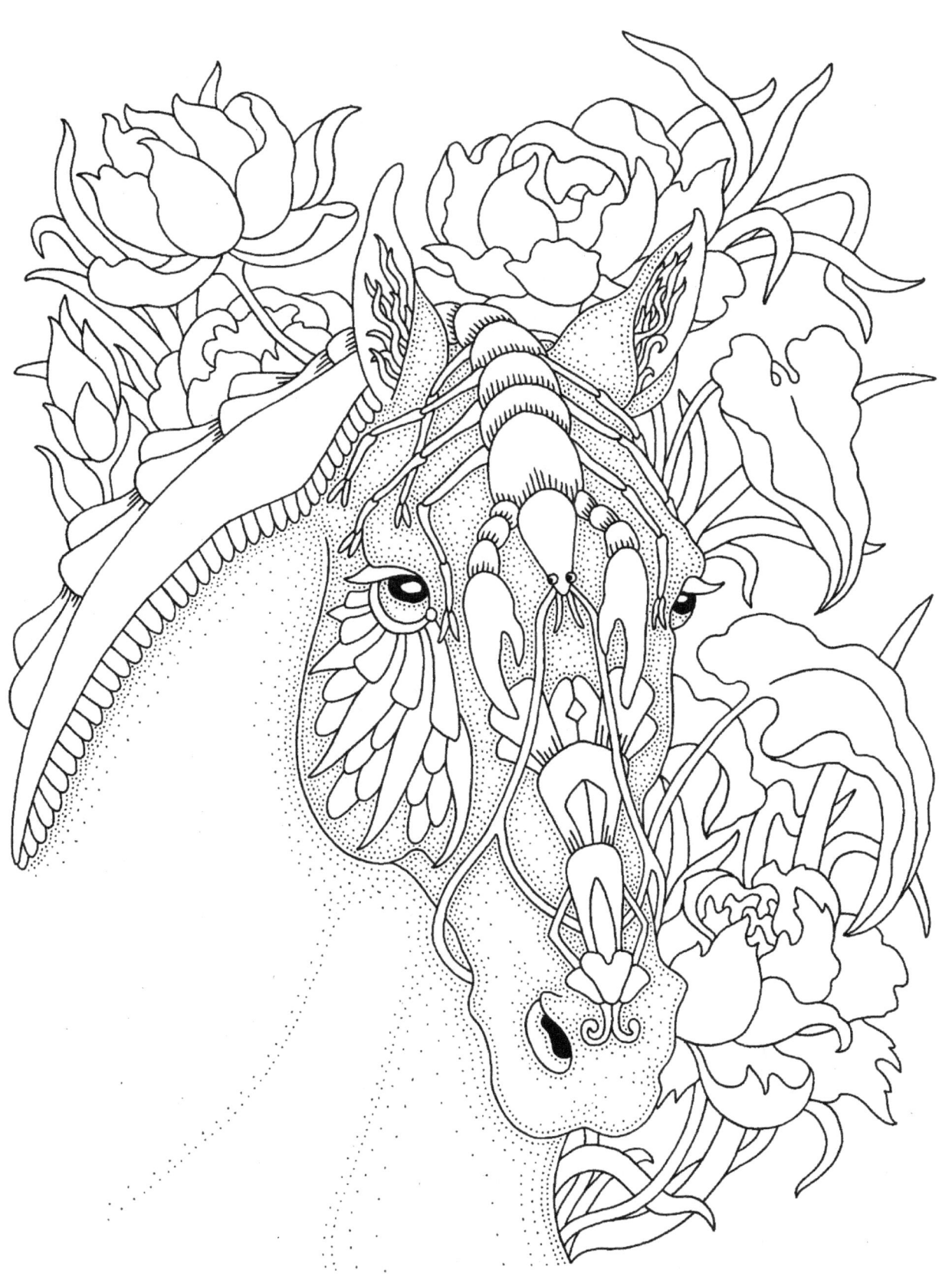

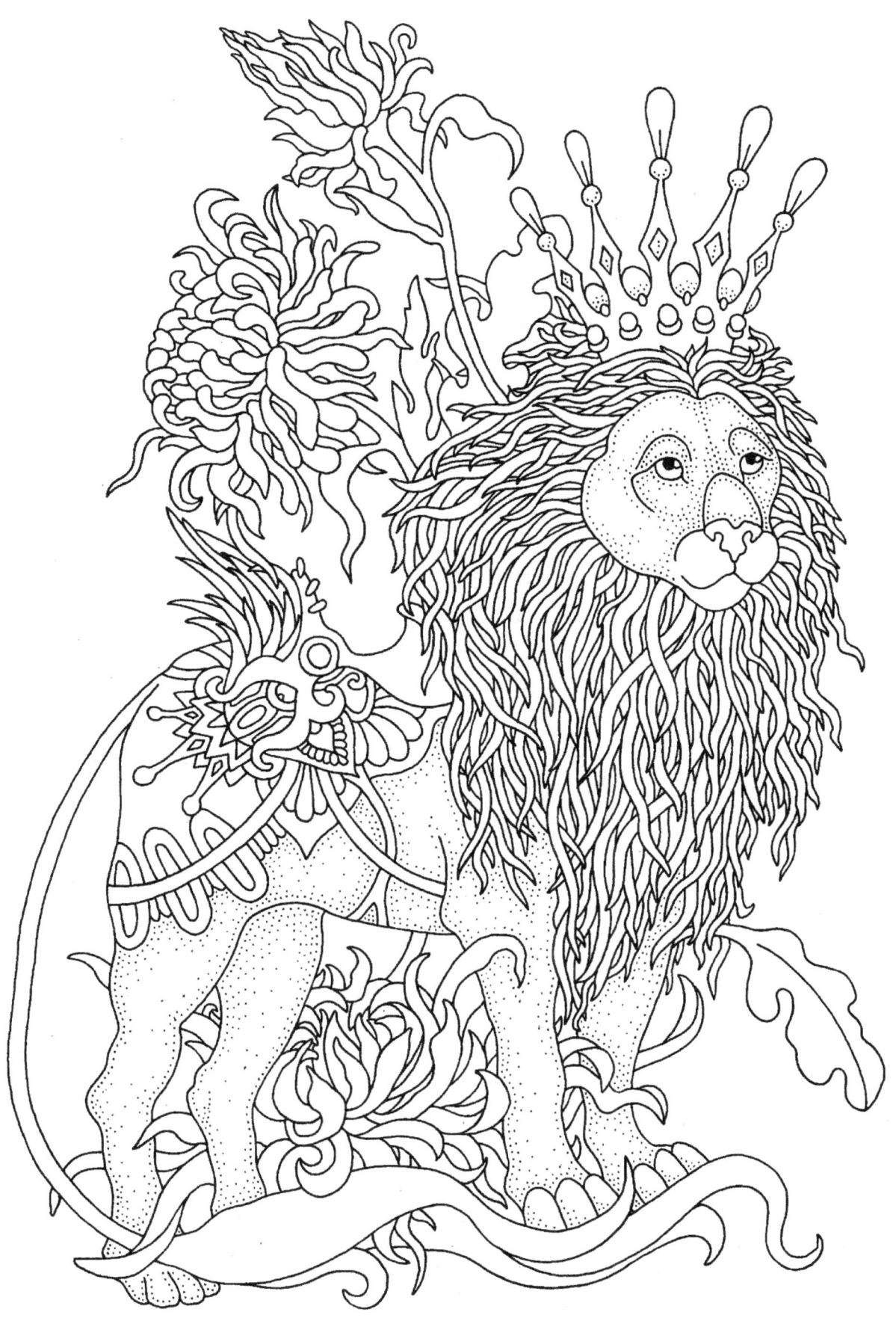

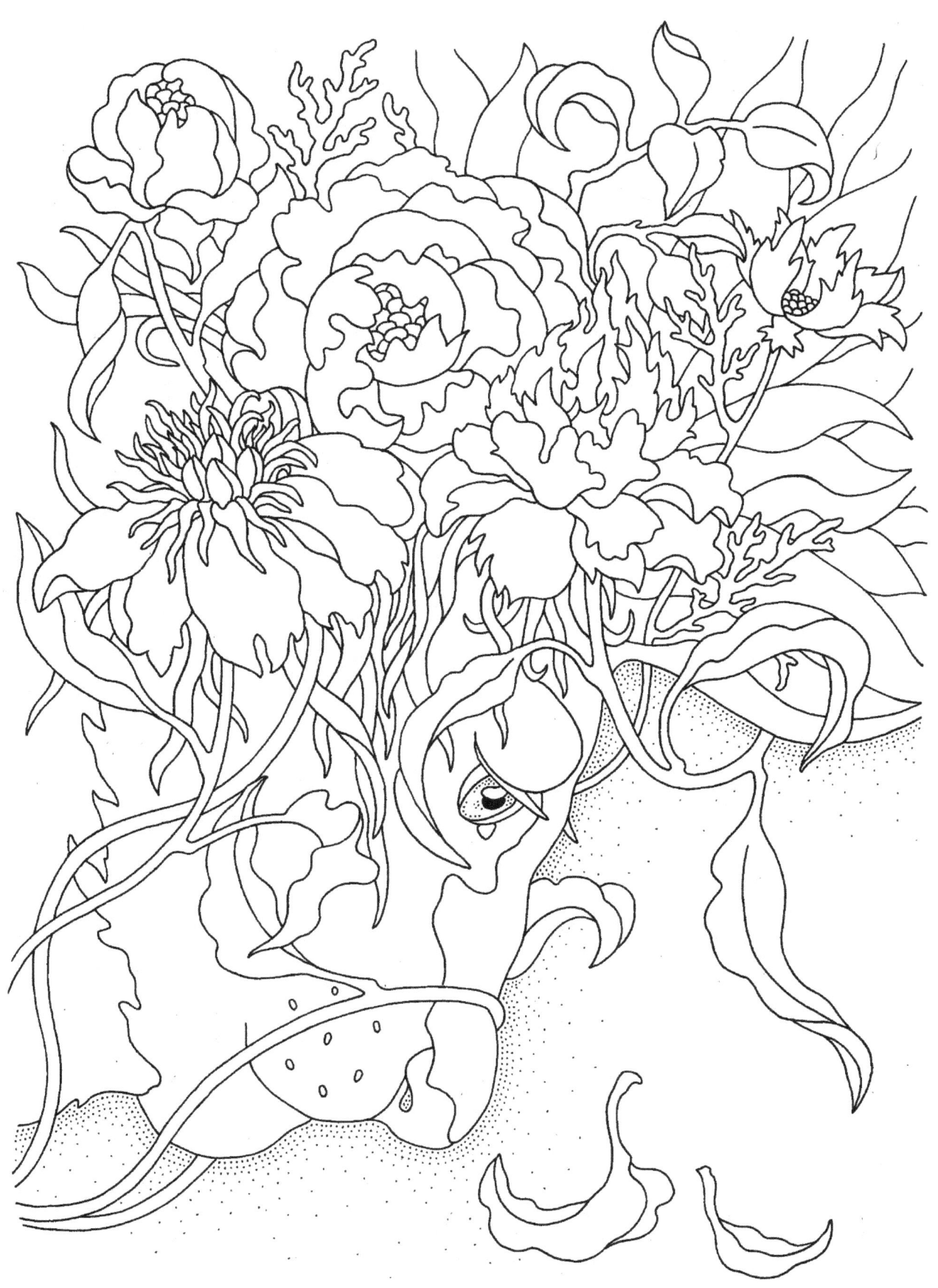

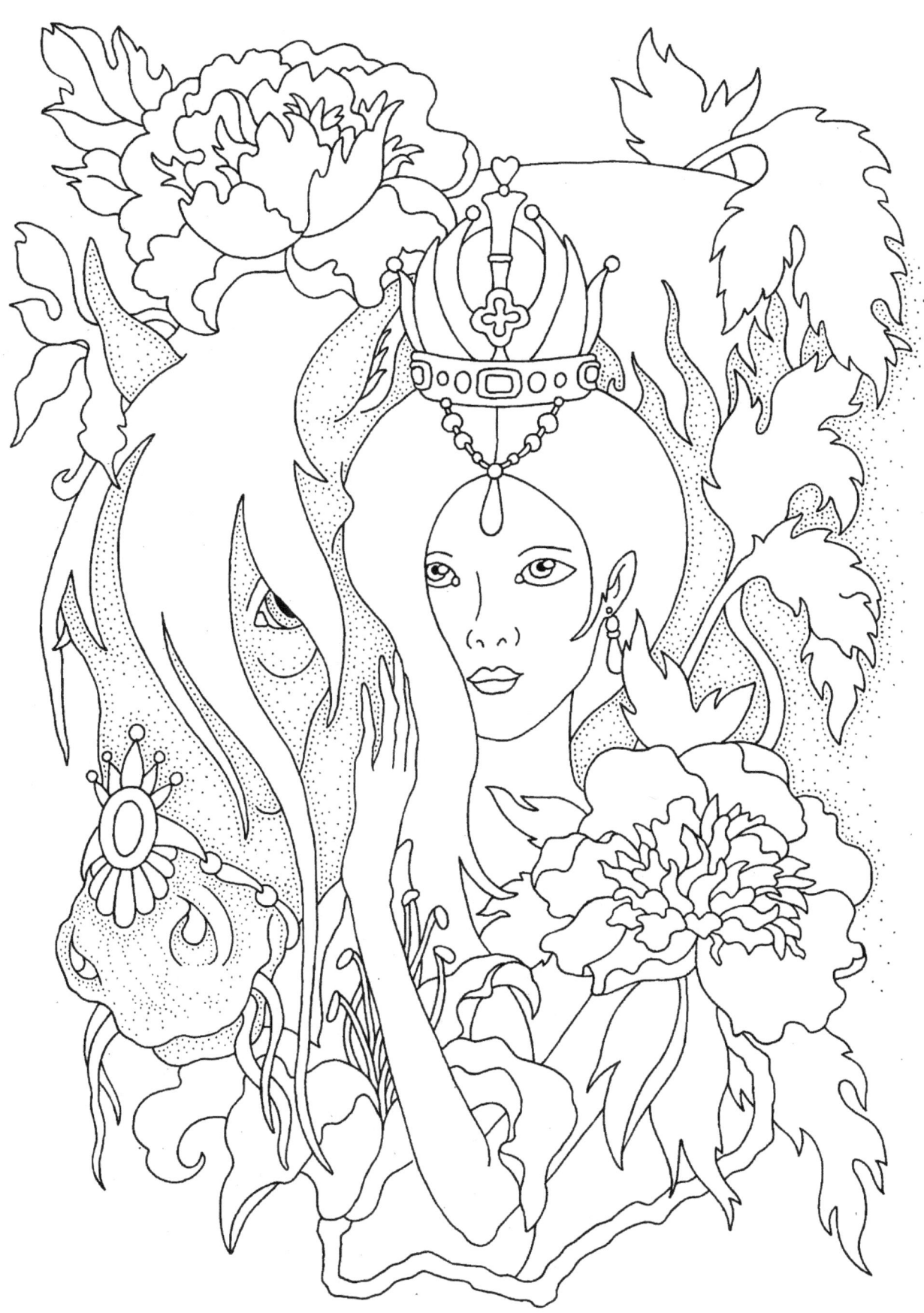

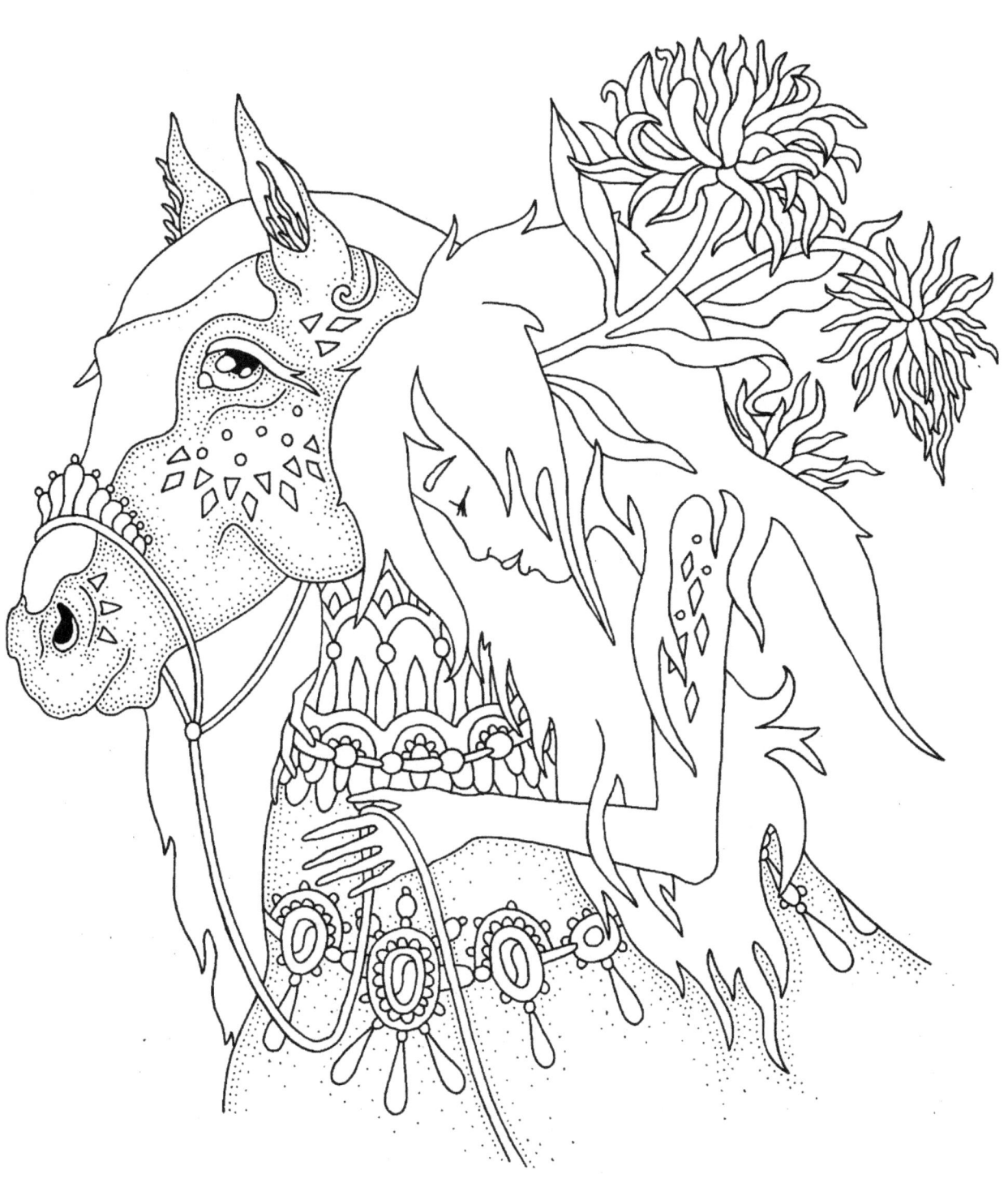

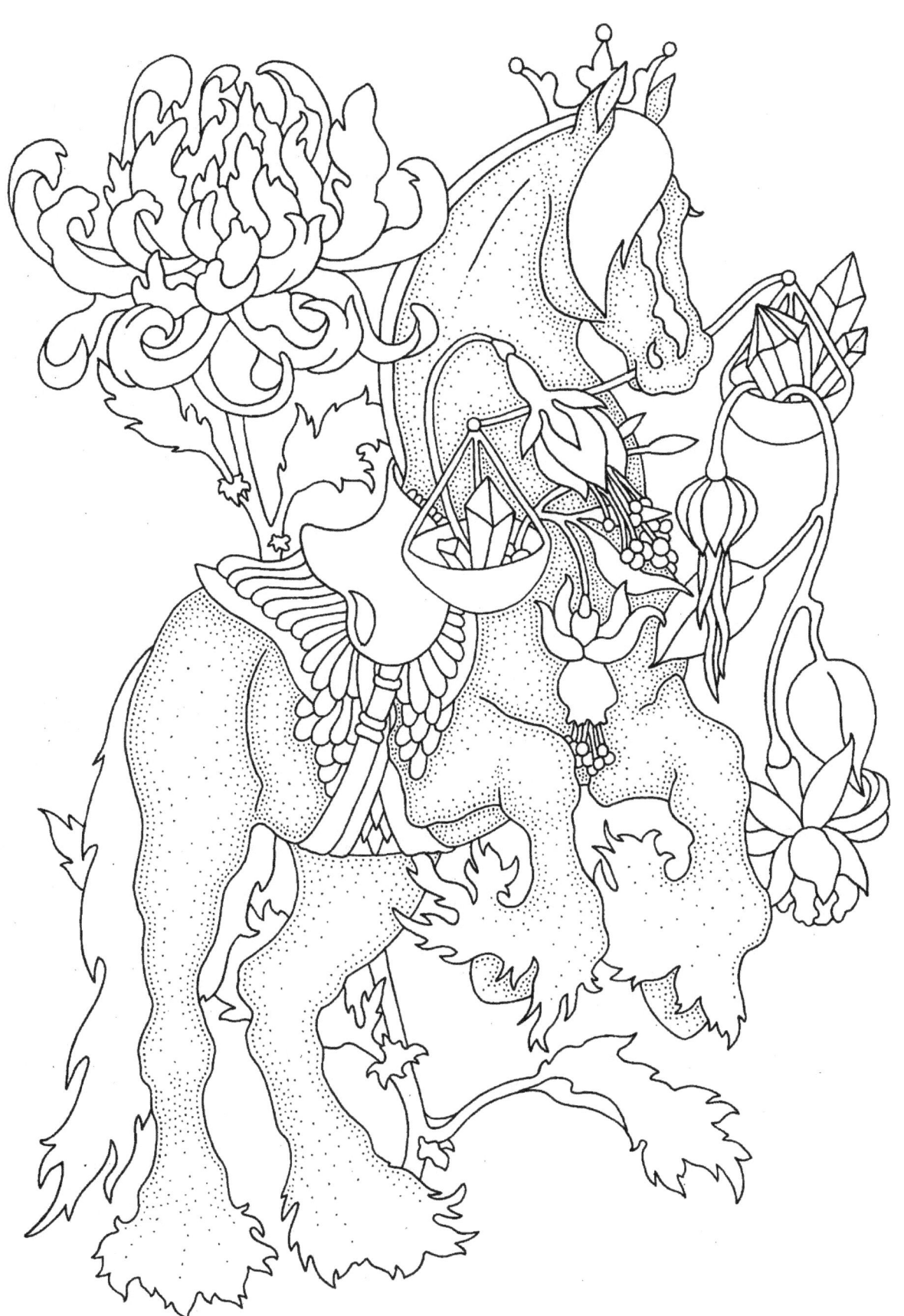

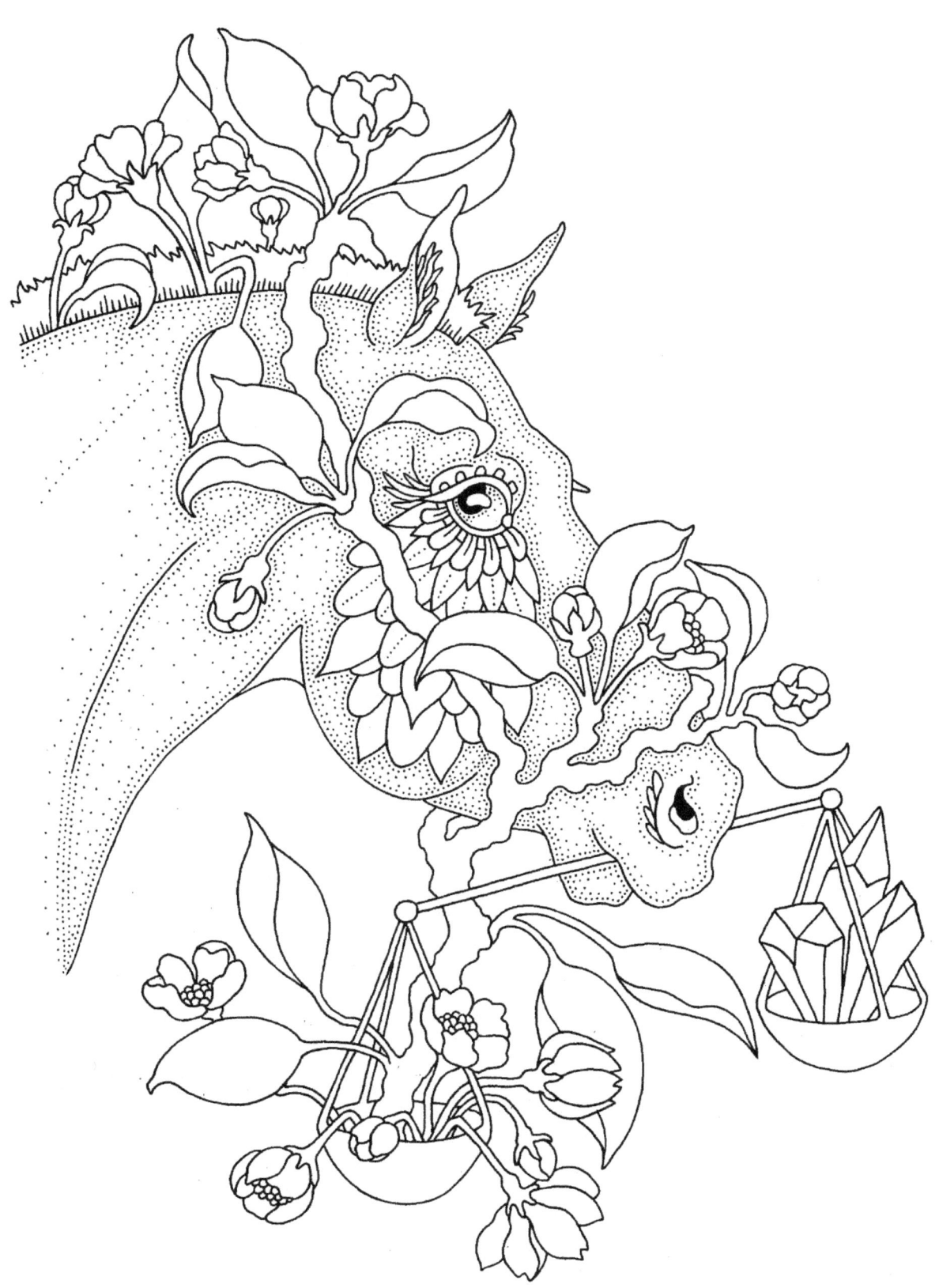

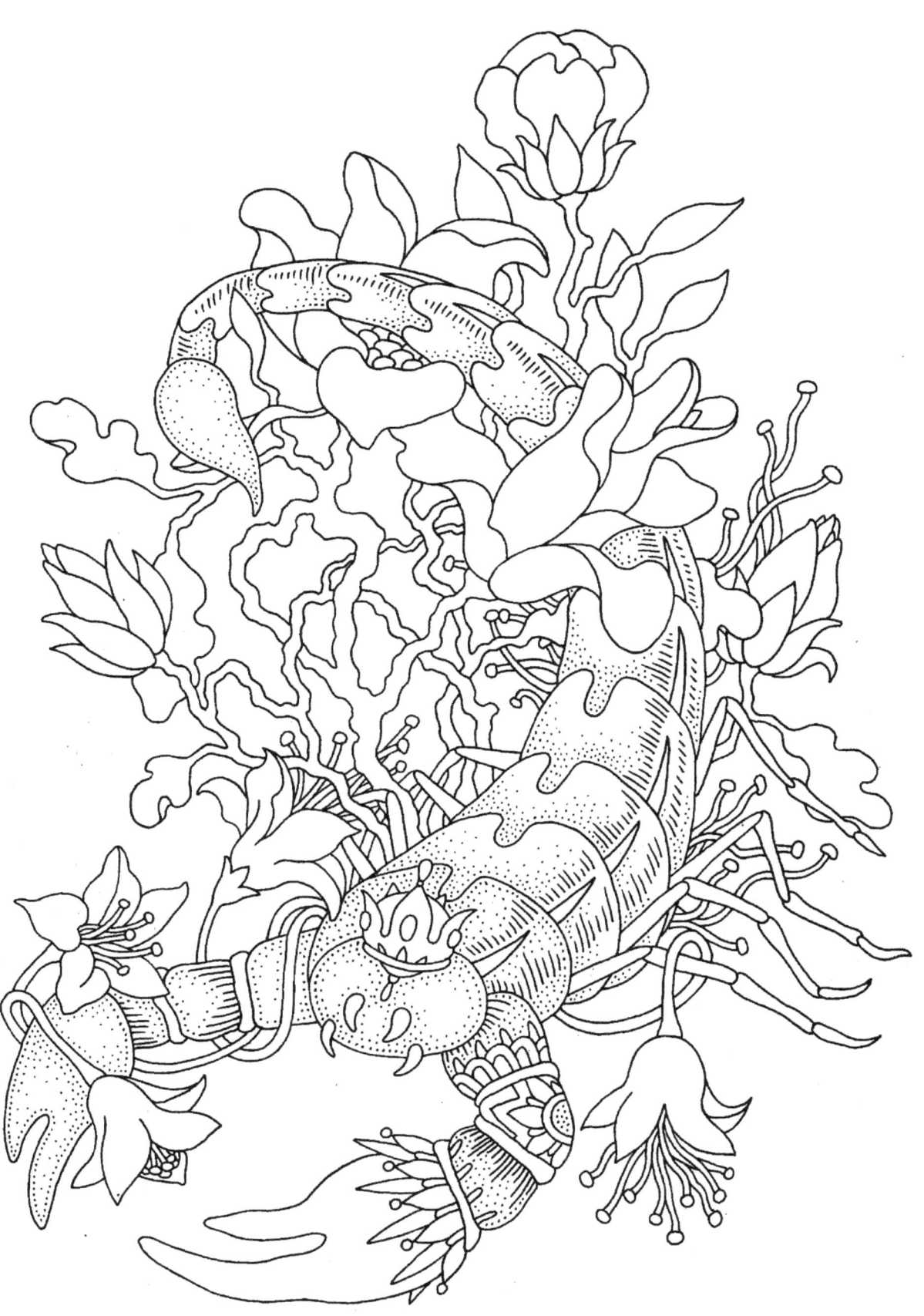

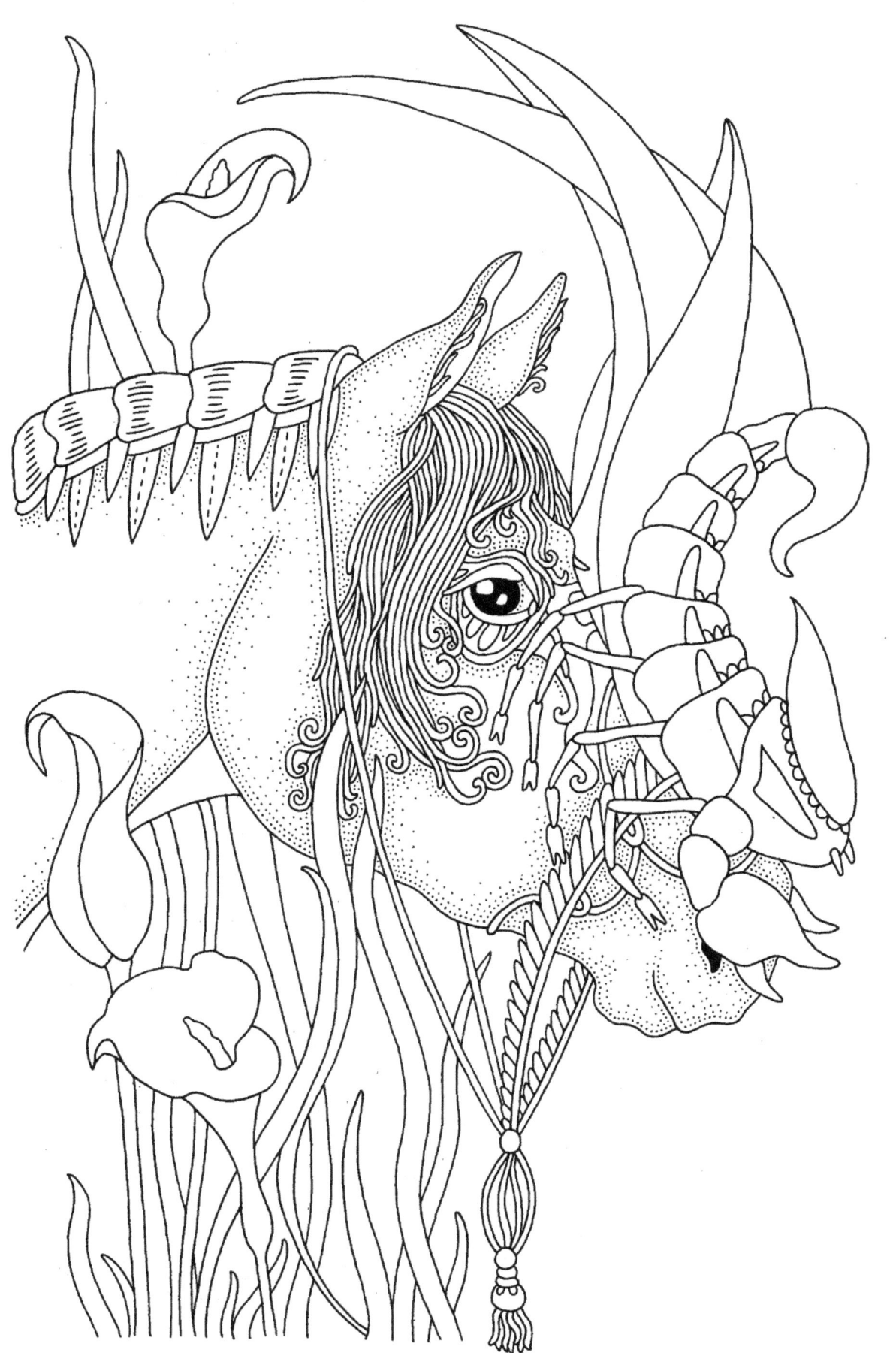

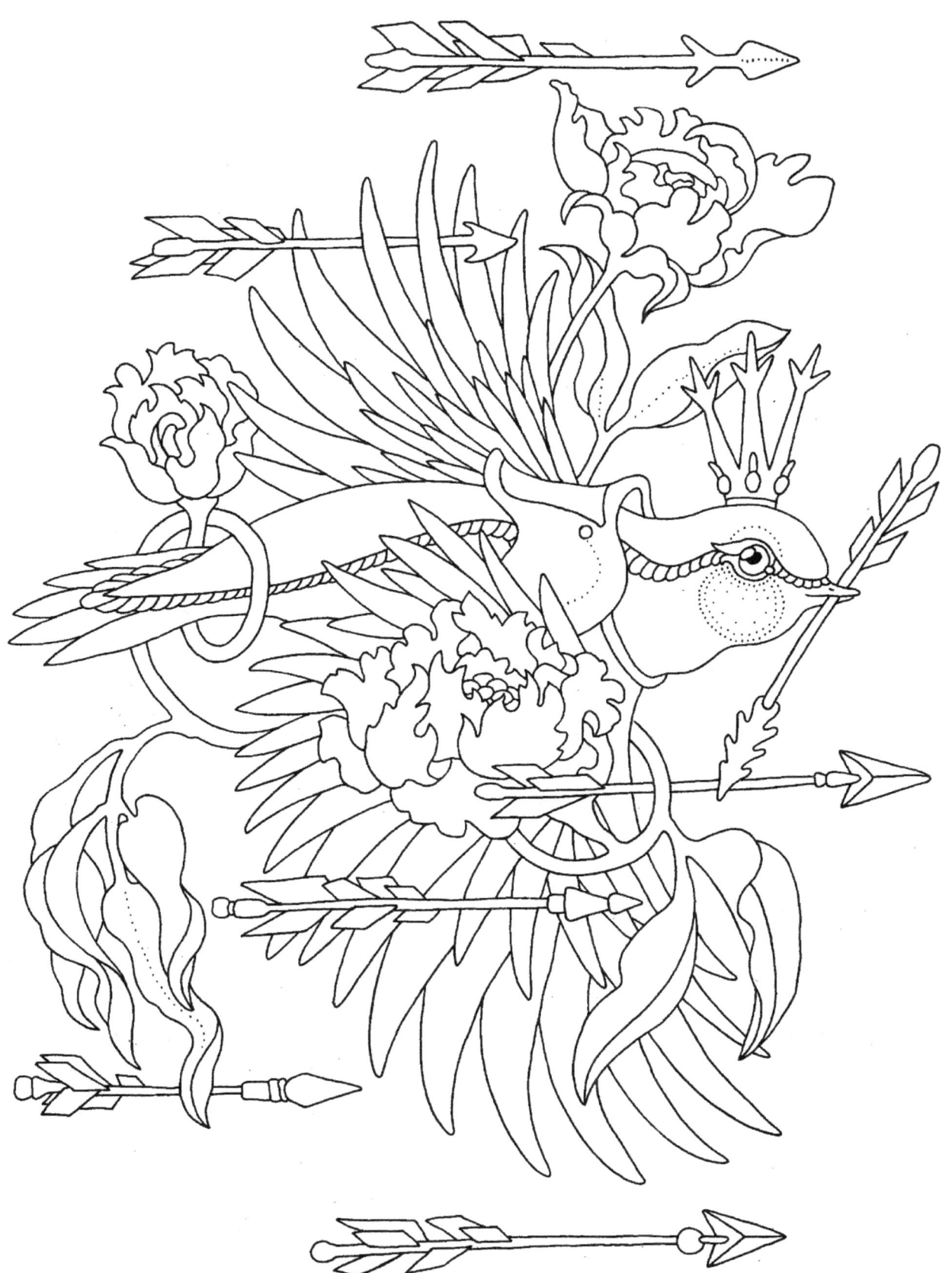

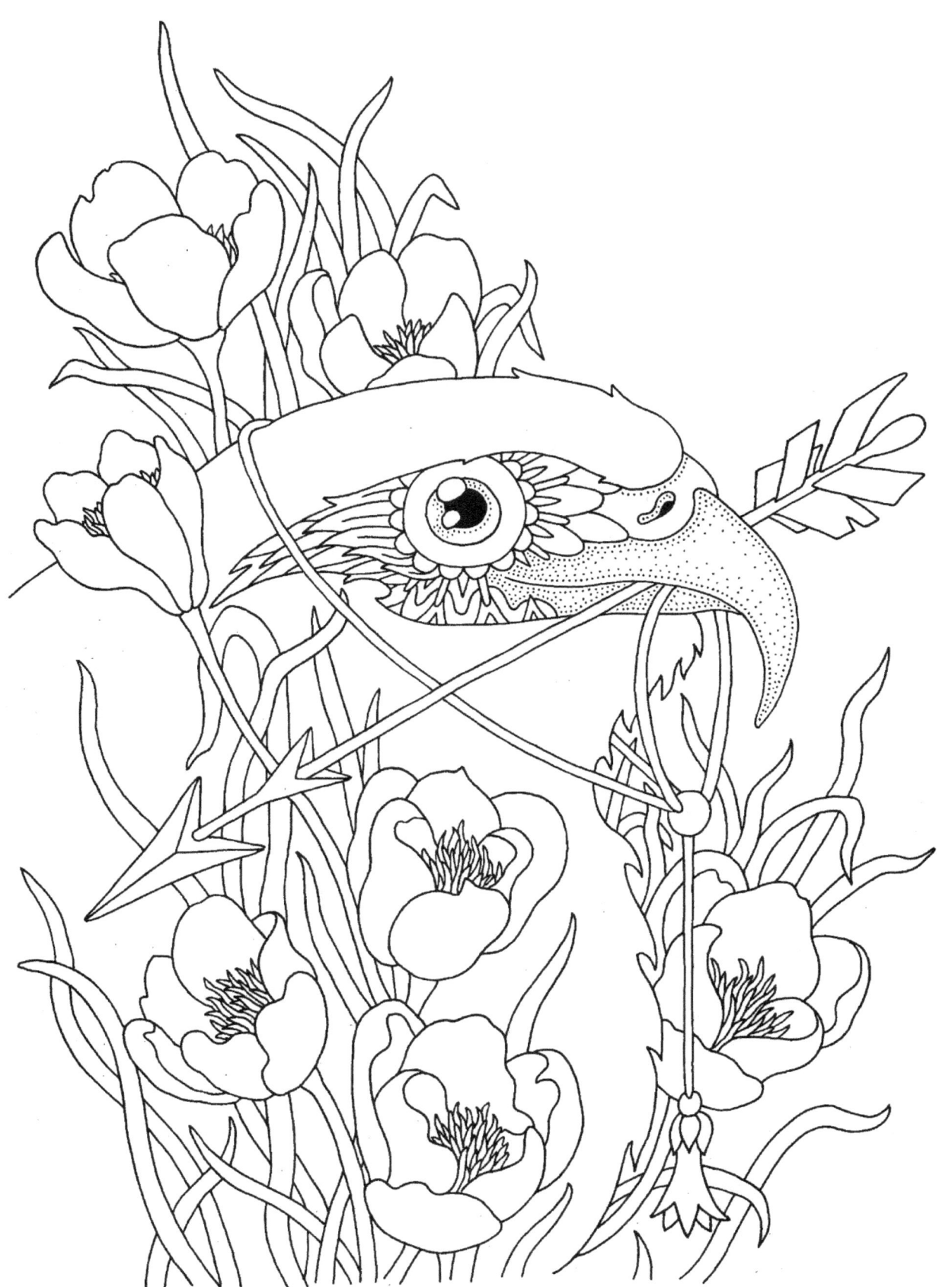

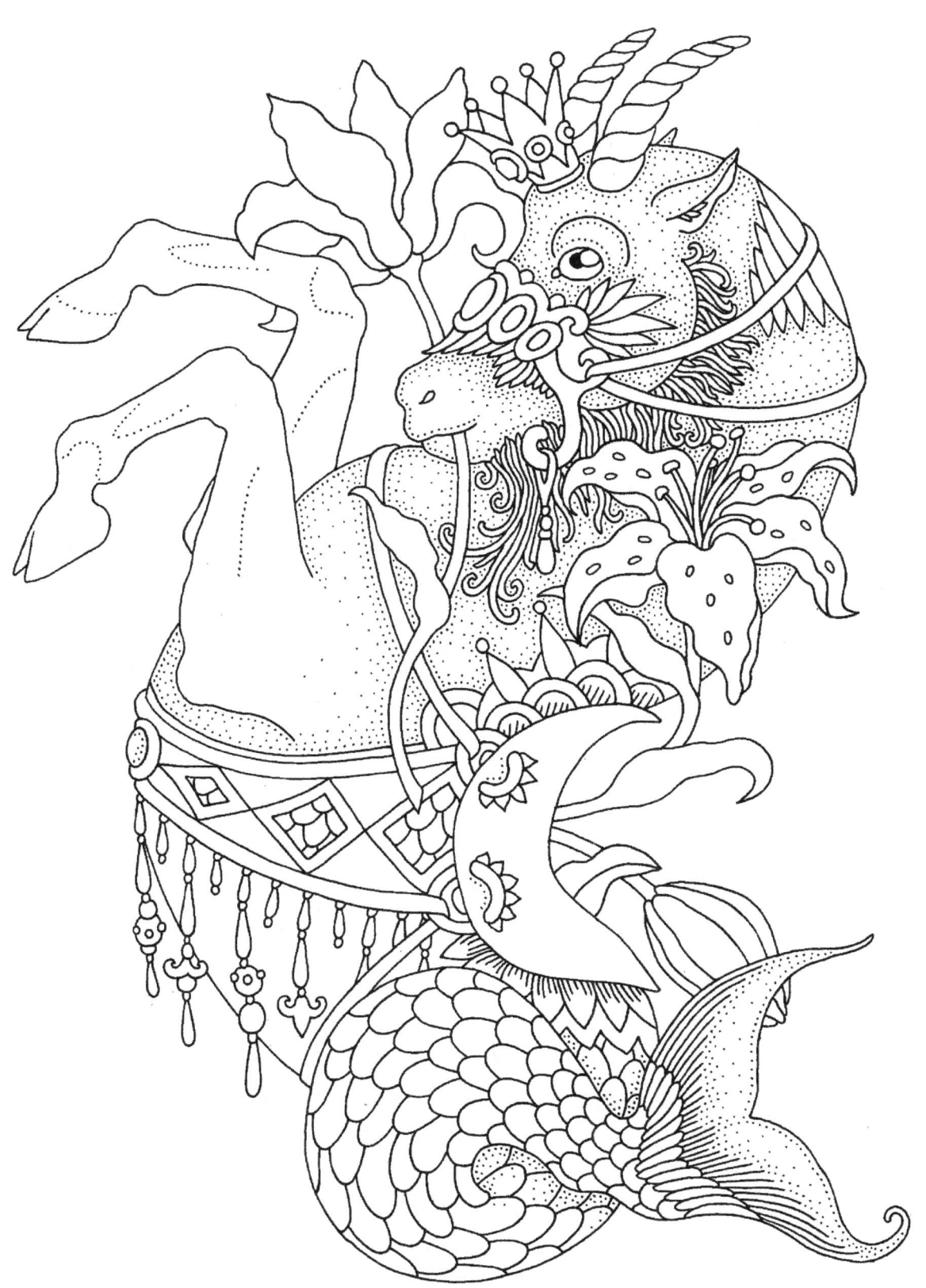

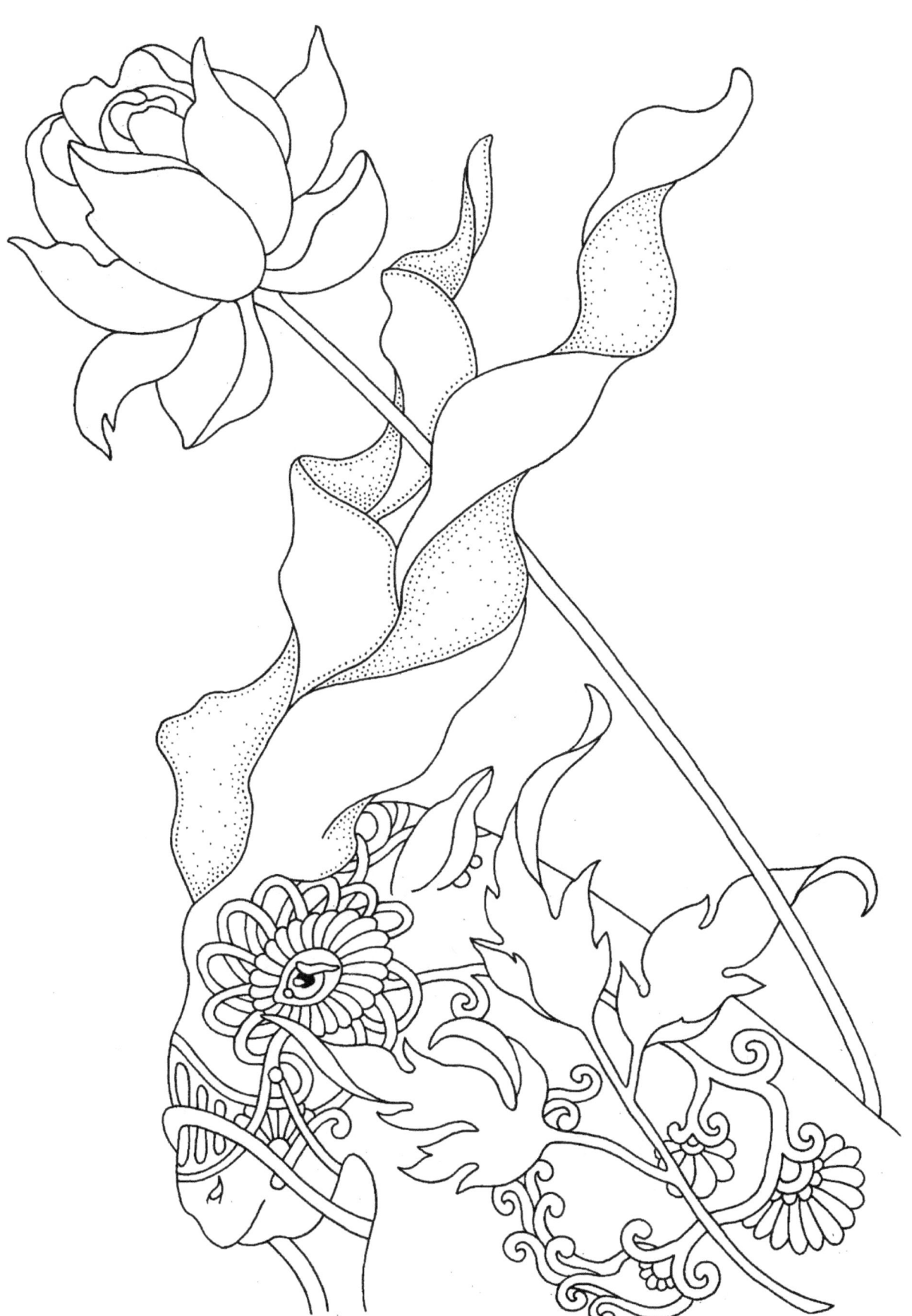

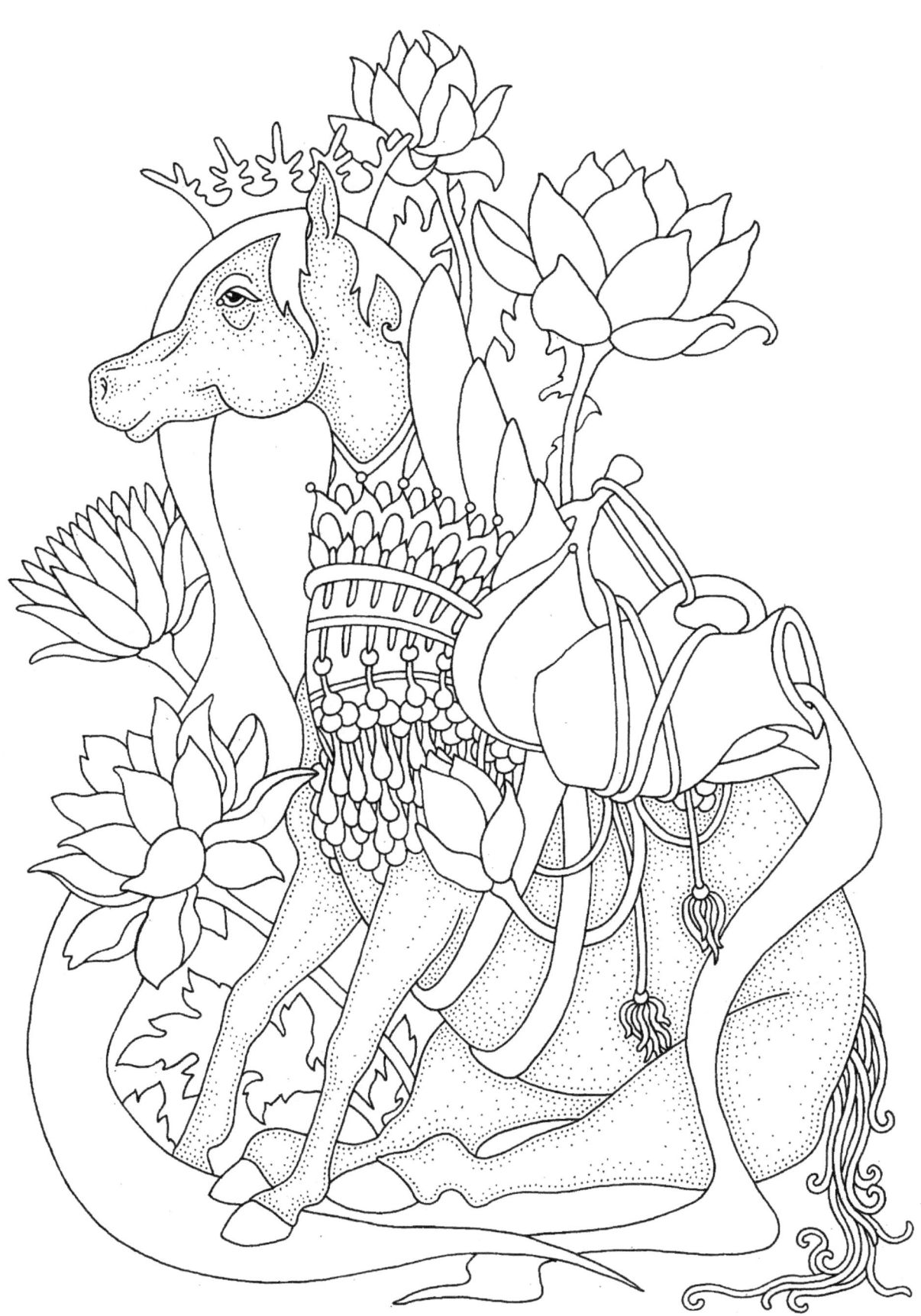

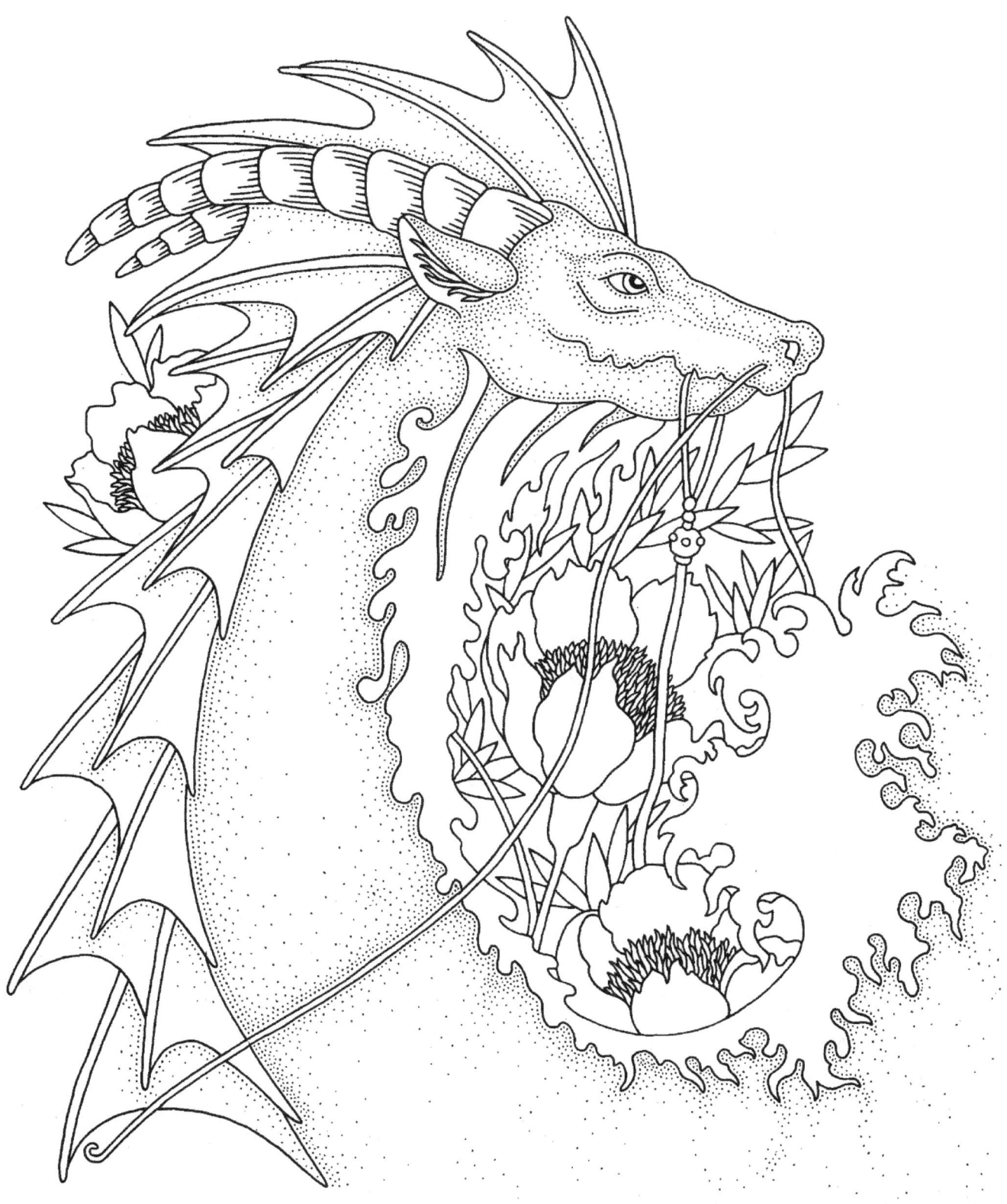

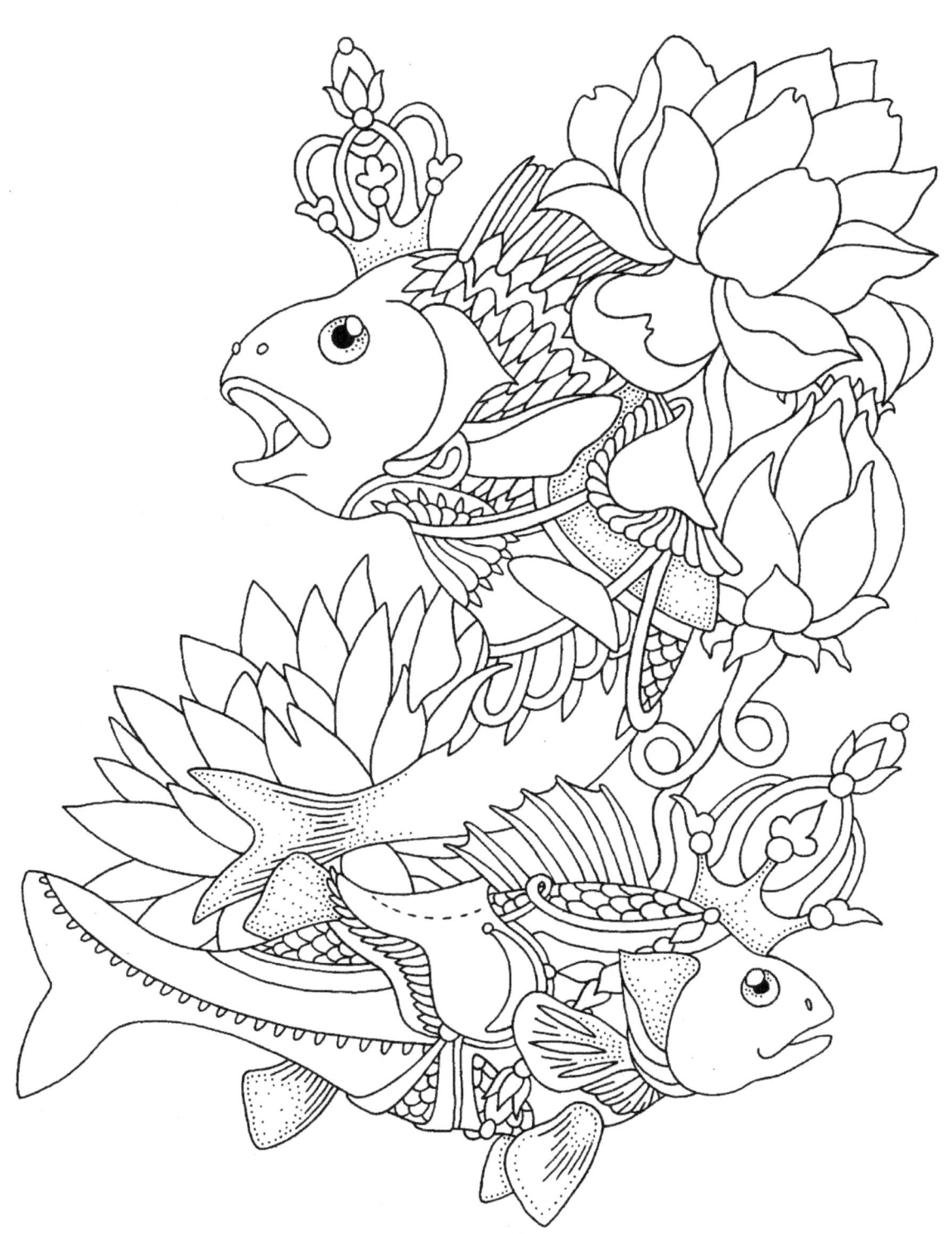

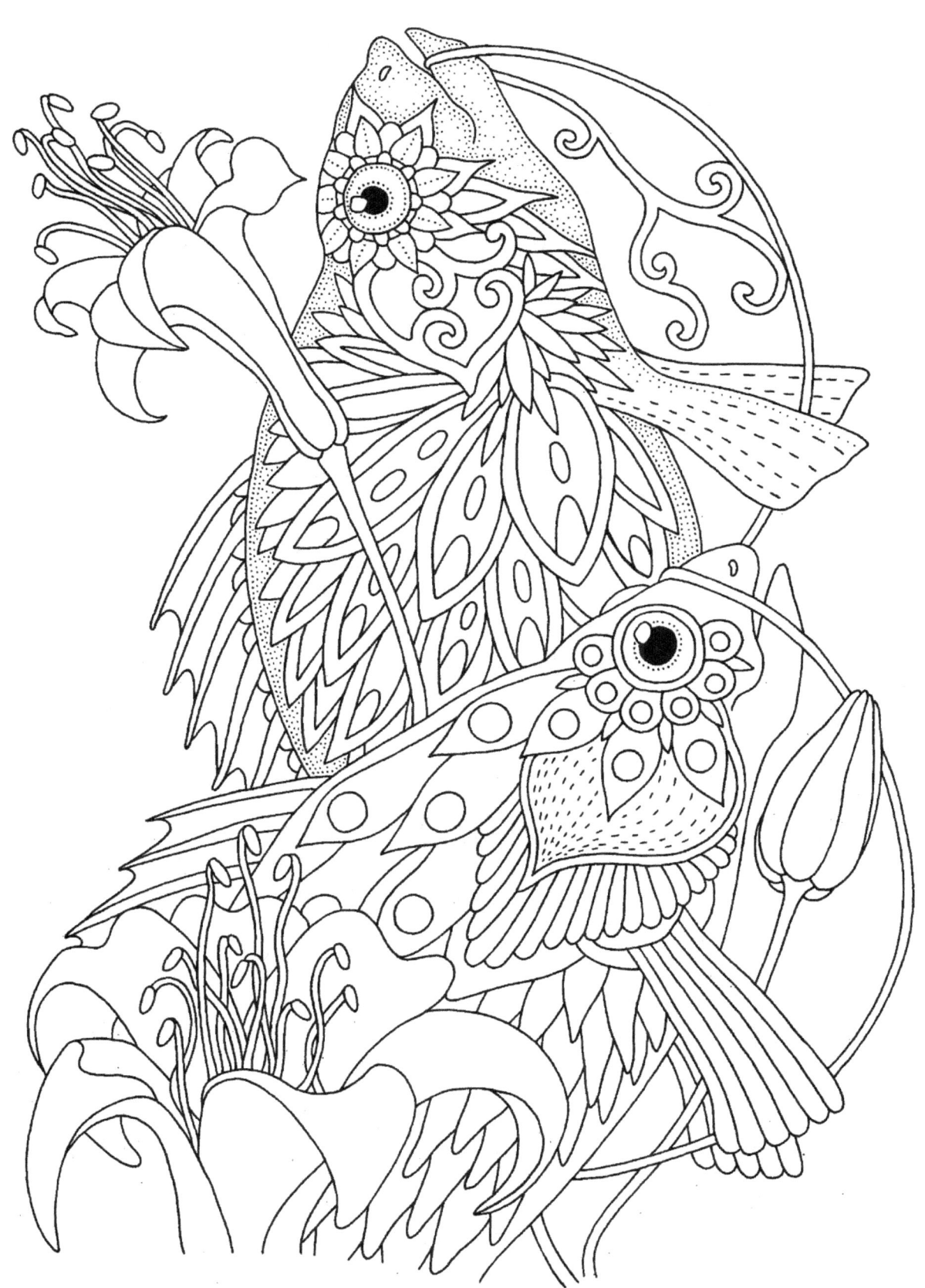

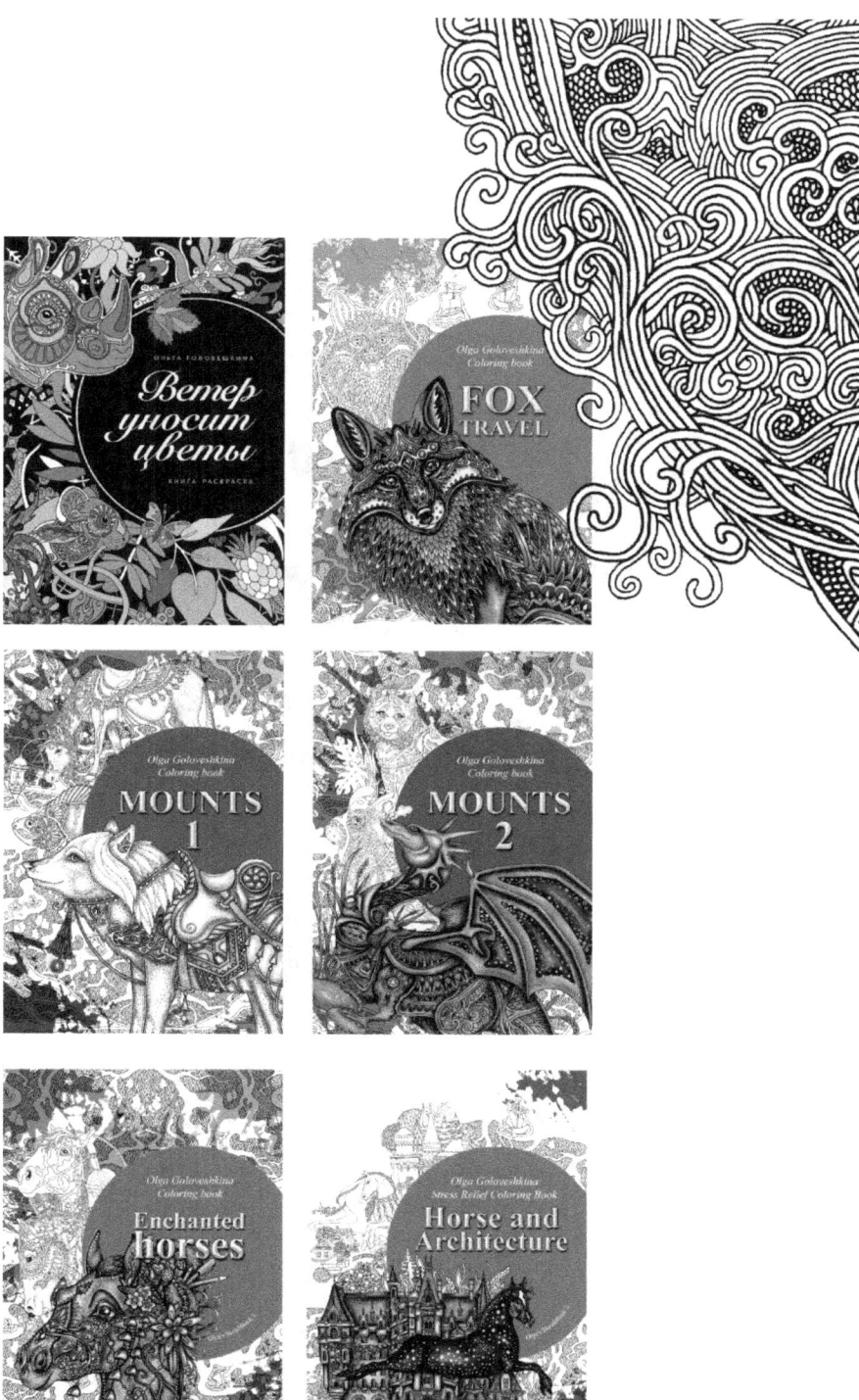

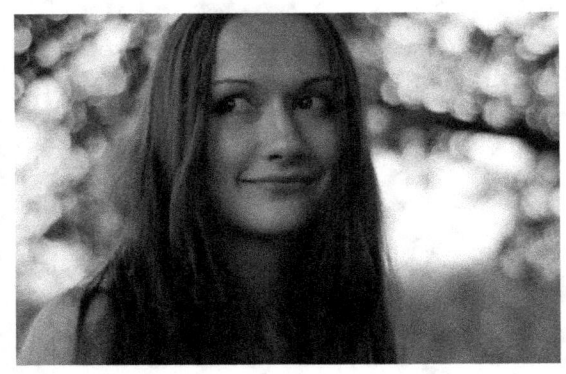

ABOUT THE AUTHOR

Olga Goloveshkina is a freelance artist and illustrator based in Moscow, Russia. She graduated from the Institute of Business and Design. Olga specializes in black ink doodles. She is an author and illustrator coloring books for adults:
1. "The wind carries flowers"/"Veter unosit tsvety" (in Russian, 2015),
2. "Fox travel: Coloring book",
3. "Mounts" (in English, 2016),
4. "Mounts 2" (in English, 2016),
5. "Enchanted horses" (in English, 2016),
6. "Horse and Architecture" (in English, 2016),
7. "Alice in Wonderland Coloring Book" (in English, 2017).

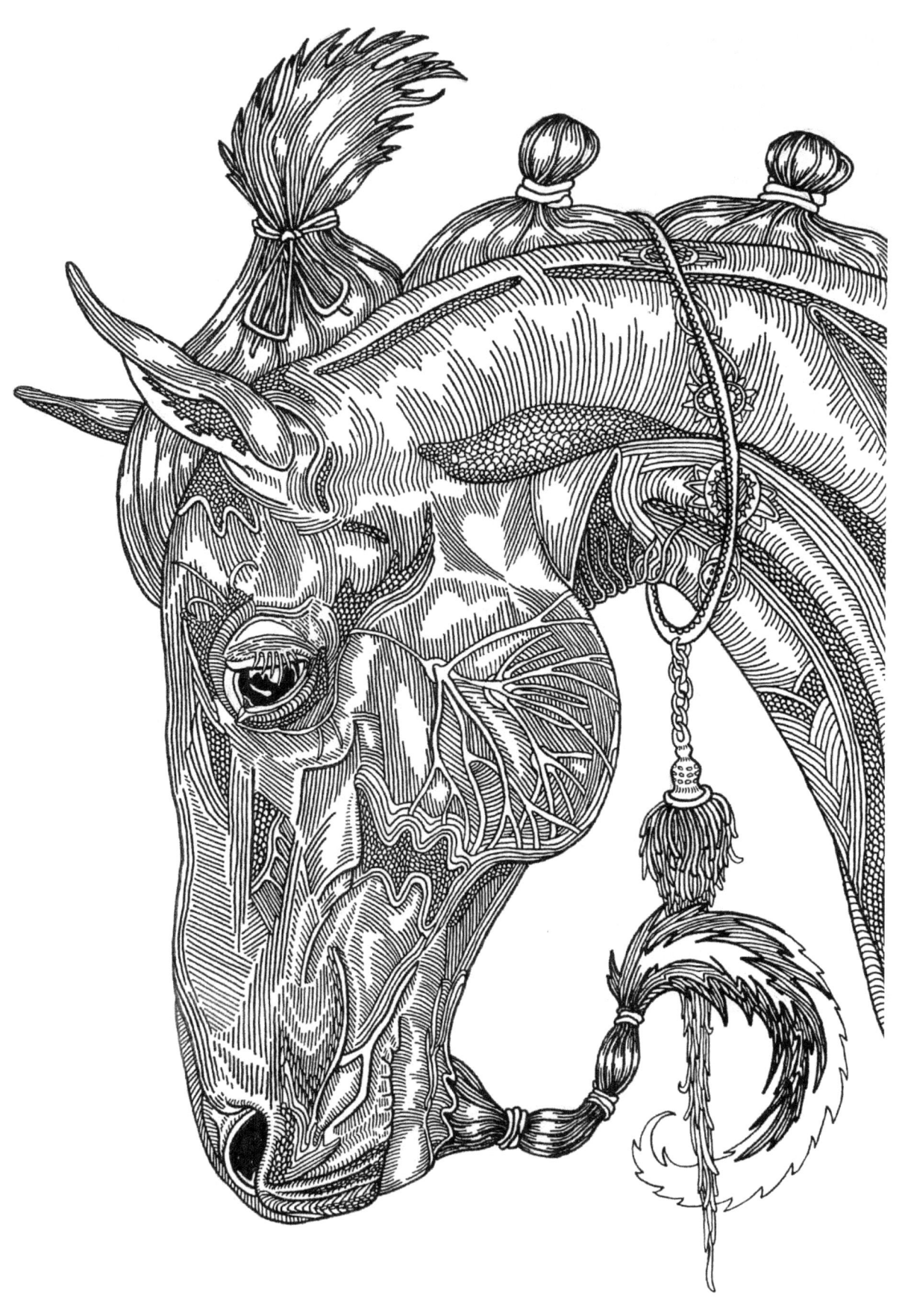

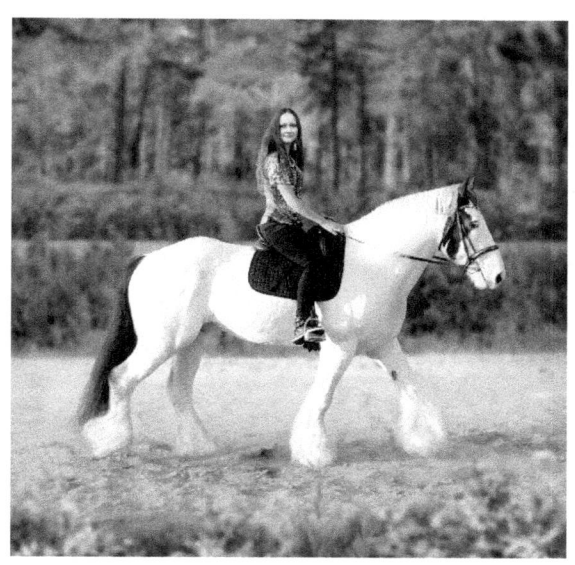

Author page on Amazon:

amazon.com/author/olgagoloveshkina

Site: http://olyagoloveshkina.jimdo.com

Instagram:

@olyahitrayapanda

www.ingramcontent.com/pod-product-compliance
Lightning Source LLC
Chambersburg PA
CBHW062200220526
45470CB00009B/2878